Dedicated to Joey and Raya,
our inspirational children.

Insects come in many shapes and sizes.

Can you guess which of these animals are insects?

Let's turn the page to find out!

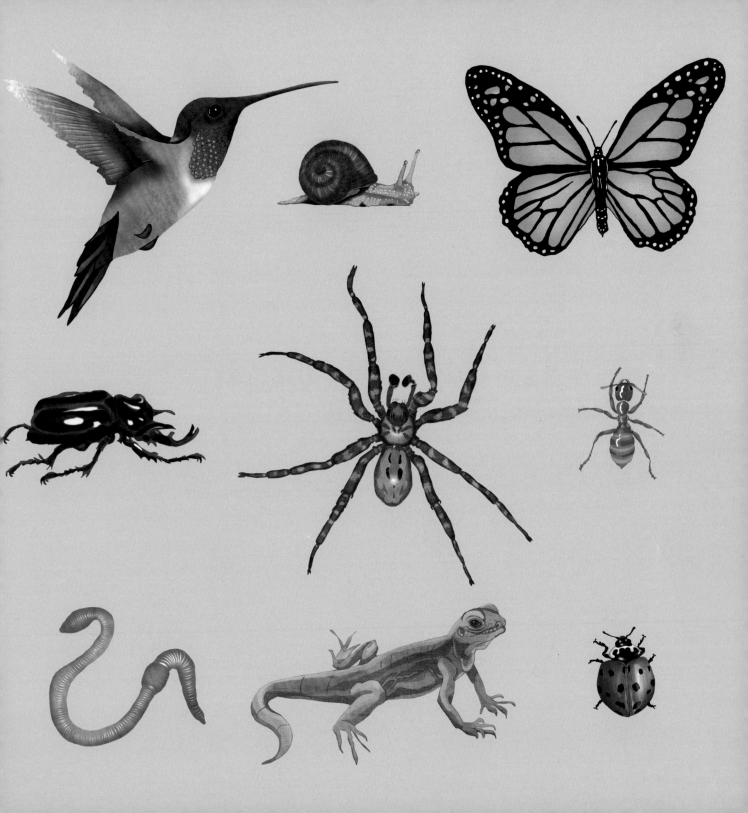

Is a ladybug an insect?

Yes!

How many legs does a ladybug have?

All insects have 6 legs.

Is a spider an insect?

No.

A spider has more than six legs.

Can you count how many?

Is a horned beetle an insect?

Yes!

All insects have hard outer bodies called exoskeletons.

*Exoskeleton:
    exo = exterior or outside
    skeleton = structure of support

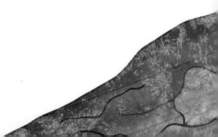

Is a lizard an insect?

No.

Lizards do not have exoskeletons, but instead they have a soft body with a skeleton inside, called an endoskeleton.

Do you have an exoskeleton or an endoskeleton?

*Endoskeleton:
    endo = interior or inside
    skeleton = structure of support

Is an ant an insect?

Yes!

How many parts of the ant's body can you find?

Insects have a 3-part body: a head, a thorax and an abdomen.

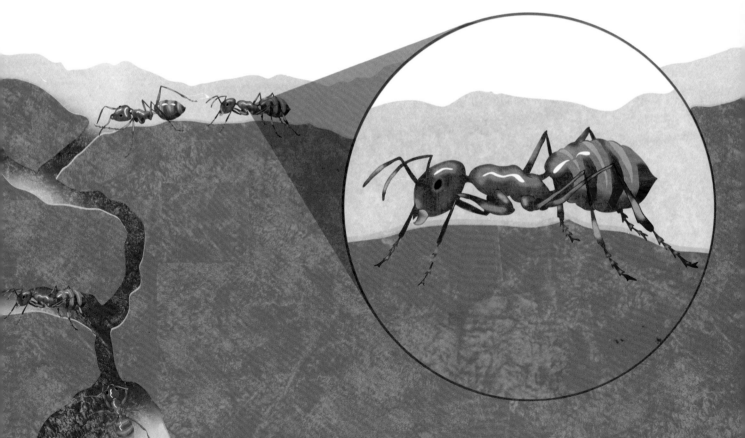

Is an earthworm an insect?

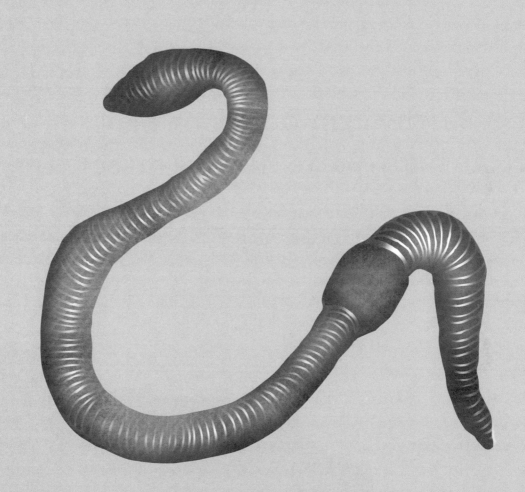

No.

An earthworm does not have
clear body parts like an insect.

Is a butterfly an insect?

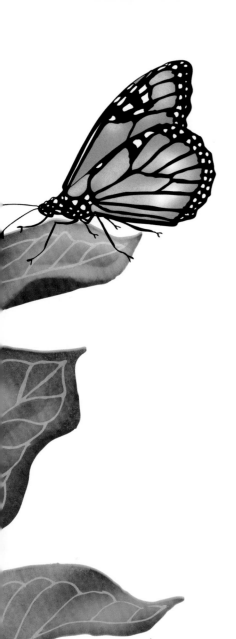

Yes!

How many pairs of wings do you see?

Winged insects have 2 pairs of wings, a top pair and a bottom pair.

Sometimes one of the pairs is very hard to find, like on flies.

Is a hummingbird an insect?

No.

Hummingbirds have only 1 pair
of wings.

Is a snail an insect?

1. **Legs**: How many legs does a snail have?

2. **Exoskeleton**: Does a snail have an exoskeleton?

3. **Body parts**: Does a snail have 3 clear body parts?

4. **Wings**: Does a snail have wings?

1. **Legs**: A snail does not have any legs.

2. **Exoskeleton**: A snail has a hard shell, but not an exoskeleton. A snail's body is soft.

3. **Body parts**: A snail does not have 3 body parts.

4. **Wings**: That's silly! A snail does not have any wings. But, not all insects have wings either.

No. A snail is not an insect.

Can you think of other characteristics that insects share? Tell us about them on our facebook page:

www.facebook.com/buddingbiologist.

For more information on each insect, and for additional teaching material, visit our website:

www.buddingbiologist.com

Hardcover printed and bound in the United States by Self Publishing, Inc. in 2013.

ISBN: 978-0-9855481-4-8